THE ARTISANAL KITCHEN

PERFECT
PASTA

Also in This Series

The Artisanal Kitchen: Perfect Pizza at Home

The Artisanal Kitchen: Vegetables the Italian Way

THE ARTISANAL KITCHEN

PERFECT PASTA

RECIPES AND SECRETS TO ELEVATE THE CLASSIC ITALIAN MEAL

ANDREW FEINBERG & FRANCINE STEPHENS
OF FRANNY'S RESTAURANT

WITH **MELISSA CLARK**

ARTISAN ■ NEW YORK

Contents

Introduction

Everyone thinks that pasta is the easiest thing in the world
to cook—you just boil up a big pot of spaghetti, drain, and
top with a premade sauce and a handful of grated cheese.
It's the last-minute dinner to end all last-minute dinners—
quick, easy, satisfying. But the very best pasta dishes are
so much more than that: truly al dente noodles that taste
of wheat, imbued with the aromatics in the sauce—be it a
few cloves of lightly browned garlic and a fat pinch of chili
flakes, some ripe tomatoes quickly warmed and glossed with
olive oil, or slowly simmered squid spiked with salty capers.
In a great pasta dish, all of the elements are integrated
and perfectly calibrated—the shape of the noodles and the
consistency of the sauce, the type and amount of cheese (if
any), the chili heat or lack thereof. They all work together to
create a blissful harmony of flavors and textures in the bowl.

Although my husband, Andrew, and I had been eating
pasta our whole lives, it wasn't until he started making it at
home in earnest, studying recipes from his favorite Italian
cookbooks (by Giuliano Bugialli, Marcella Hazan, and Fred
Plotkin), that we started to fully appreciate the differences
between a perfectly good pasta dish and a phenomenal one.
Ingredients are key, of course. But so is technique. And
one of the most important pasta lessons that Andrew ever
learned was a classic Italian method for cooking pasta that,
for some reason, is not embraced in the United States.

It might be because it's slightly more complicated than the
American standard of boil-drain-pour-on-the-marinara. In

the States, the first time the pasta meets the sauce is when you twirl it all together with a fork. There is no real unity of flavors—and the noodles are usually overcooked and limp. This is definitely not the case in Italy, where one of the hallmarks of a properly cooked pasta dish is al dente noodles that are seasoned fully with the flavors of the sauce.

Achieving this pasta perfection is a two-step process (see Pasta Techniques, pages 36–37, for more details). Step 1 is to undercook the pasta by about 2 minutes. This ensures that the pasta maintains an essential spine of chewiness. Step 2 is to finish cooking the noodles in the sauce, which, ideally, you've been simmering in a skillet on another burner. Finishing the pasta in the sauce gives the noodles a chance to meld with and absorb all the good flavors in the pan. It makes for a deeper-tasting dish in which all the ingredients are wedded into a well-balanced whole. It takes practice to get the timing down (you'll need to get to know different shapes and brands of pasta), but once you do, the pasta will emerge supple, intensely flavored, and with a toothsome bite.

Andrew started cooking pasta like this at home way before we opened our restaurant, Franny's, but we quickly discovered that it was one thing to be able to make, say, a great *cacio e pepe* in our home kitchen, and another thing entirely to do it consistently in a very busy restaurant. After a few months of struggling, we decided to take pasta off the menu until we could remodel the kitchen and put in a proper pasta tank, which we did in a few years. But in your kitchen, the Italian two-step method should work well, and we highly recommend giving it a try, adapting your own favorite pasta recipes, as well as the ones in this book.

Most of the recipes you'll find here are based on Italian classics that we've altered to some degree. Andrew always strives to keep the core elements of the original dish intact. His tweaks are subtle, like adding a touch of shrimp stock to bring out the sweet sea flavor in his Spaghettini with Shrimp (page 33) or using aromatic Meyer lemons in his *alla limone* (see page 82). He makes a version of *puttanesca* (see page 41) that omits the tomato but ramps up the flavor of the other ingredients (anchovies, capers, garlic) by browning them thoroughly. For the most part, he leaves well enough alone. Cooks in Italy know what they are doing.

This is also true when it comes to ingredients. In Italy, it's pretty easy to find high-quality pasta made by small artisanal producers in every little supermarket. Luckily, these pastas are becoming more and more available here too. Pasta from artisan producers might cost more, but supporting a true craftsman is well worth the higher price tag, especially since you end up with an excellent product. Frequently the business has been family-run for generations; perhaps the wheat is grown near the same village where the pasta is produced. That pricey bag of artisanal Italian pasta may reflect the livelihood and pride of an entire community. With all that heritage, tradition, and expertise going for it, how could it not be superior?

For dry pasta, we like to buy from the Campania region, where many of the best Italian pasta producers are located. A town called Gragnano, near Naples, has seven or eight amazing artisanal pasta makers alone.

Italian artisanal dry pasta is made with *grano duro* (hard-grain) durum wheat. It has a golden yellow color and is extruded through rugged bronze dies that in many cases have been in use for decades or longer. It's slowly air-dried for a minimum of 24 hours (and up to 72 hours), helping to make it dense and resilient. Sauce adheres perfectly to its porous, textured surface, and thanks to its density, the pasta holds its shape and toothsome character after cooking.

Industrially made dry pasta, on the other hand, is shoved through Teflon-coated dies, a process that greatly speeds up extrusion and production but results in a reedy, slick (nonstick) noodle. Commercial pasta is also made from a more yielding, cheaper strain of wheat, and it is rapidly dried with heaters, essentially parcooking the noodles. Large-scale industrially made pasta is inferior to artisanal pasta in all respects: it breaks down in water, becoming flabby and mushy, and sauce slides away from its slippery surface.

If you take the time to track down the best pasta and other ingredients and then use the two-step pasta cooking method, you're pretty much guaranteed a fantastic meal. But there are a few final touches that can make it even better, such as finishing a skillet full of well-sauced pasta with an emulsifying spoonful of butter, a fragrant splash of olive oil, a sprinkle of creamy cheese, or a combination of all three. Then, once the pasta is plated, a drizzle of olive oil and maybe a little very coarsely grated cheese will make all the flavors pop. At the end, when you're finished with your meal, you should have no more than a few teaspoons of pasta sauce at the bottom—just enough for a single swipe of your bread to finish everything off.

—Francine Stephens

COOKING NOTES

Great cooking is so much more than just following a recipe. Here are some tips and pointers that will make all your homemade meals—whether from this book or not—even better.

Eat Seasonally and Locally

The wonderful thing about eating seasonally is that without question, your food will be more flavorful. Cooking seasonally makes shopping easier, because you'll know that what you're getting is fresh. The cauliflower and kale that you can find in January are far better ingredients for your cooking in winter than pale, mealy tomatoes. Yet really ripe summer tomatoes are so remarkable that you need to do very little to them, and even a simple tomato salad can be extraordinary. The more local those tomatoes, the less distance they have had to travel and the riper they probably are. If you're lucky enough to have a farmers' market nearby, take advantage of it. It's hands down the best place to source seasonal, fresh, local ingredients. Plus, shopping at the farmers' market can be a rewarding experience—you can look your farmer in the eye, and you are directly subsidizing the people responsible for feeding you and your family (you don't get that kind of satisfaction in a supermarket).

Explore new produce that you may be unfamiliar with: farmers' markets and CSAs (community-supported agriculture) provide great avenues for experimentation. If you enjoy cucumbers, try a Tasty Jade or lemon cucumber instead of the Kirbys you usually buy. Tuscan black kale cooks just like its green cousin, but it has a slightly earthier flavor. Buying different heirloom varieties of vegetables that you might already be familiar with can be a great way to expand your cooking horizons.

Farmers' markets are fun, joyous places full of bounty and grateful shoppers, who themselves can be a resource. Don't be shy about asking folks around you about the things they're selling or the things they're buying. Talk to the farmers, and ask them what they do with the mizuna they're offering. Talk to other shoppers—ask the fellow in line ahead of you how he plans to cook those sunchokes. And, of course, there's always the Internet: if you don't know what to do with the gorgeous green garlic you lugged home, there's a website that will tell you.

Use High-Quality Ingredients

Many of the recipes in this book are very simple, with only a few ingredients, so it's important to make sure those ingredients are of the best quality you can find. Using real Parmigiano-Reggiano is a must—any other "Parmesan" just won't have the same flavor. A high-quality extra-virgin olive oil can make any recipe exceptional. Artisanally made dry pasta is vastly superior to most of the large-scale, industrially made pasta we're all familiar with. And good olive-oil-packed anchovies or Italian salt-cured anchovies are the only way to go. If you stock your pantry with great ingredients, you'll always have an excellent meal at the ready. Spaghetti with White Puttanesca (page 71) is a perfect example of a lovely, quick dinner that can be put together right out of your pantry. And while some of the products we recommend may be more expensive than what you're used to buying, they're absolutely worth it.

Keep a Well-Stocked Pantry

Build your pantry slowly, piece by piece, and be sure to restock your favorites. The essentials listed below will bring your cooking to another level. The Resources section (page 89) tells you where to purchase high-quality ingredients if you can't find them where you live.

- Extra-virgin olive oil, preferably a few different styles (such as a peppery Sicilian and a buttery Ligurian)
- High-quality olive-oil-packed anchovies
- Italian artisanal dry pasta, both short shapes and long (such as penne and spaghetti)
- Good dried chilies, preferably a few different types (such as chile de árbol and Controne)
- Dried beans, including cannellini and chickpeas
- Capers, both salt-packed and brined
- Canned D.O.P.-certified San Marzano tomatoes
- Vinegars: white wine, red wine, balsamic, and moscato
- Fresh shelled whole nuts such as walnuts, almonds, pistachios, and pine nuts (the oils in nuts are perishable, so buy from shops that have a high turnover and store the nuts in your refrigerator)
- King Arthur or other high-quality all-purpose flour
- Dried oregano, preferably Italian
- Fresh garlic
- Bread crumbs, preferably homemade
- A few different varieties of good olives, such as dark, briny Gaetas and fruity Castelvetranos

Simple Is Better

With great basics on hand, you can simply add a few fresh ingredients—for example, sausage, cheese, and broccoli rabe—and create a spectacular bowl of pasta like Maccheroni with Pork Sausage and Broccoli Rabe (page 23) without a lot of kitchen prep. Once you have the best ingredients you can find, you won't need to do much to them. Keeping a dish simple means that you can really savor those little pops of sausage, the creamy sharpness of the cheese, and the bitter bite of the broccoli rabe.

Simplicity is one of the hallmarks of *cucina povera*, which inspired many of the recipes in this book. *Cucina povera* (literally "poverty cuisine") gets the most flavor possible out of a particular ingredient, and it also gets the most out of the ingredient, period. Many of us don't use up an entire loaf of good bread at one meal, but why let that heel go to waste? Turn it into bread crumbs or into rustic croutons to add to Penne with Spicy Cauliflower (page 62). And for our sweet and flavorful Penne with Broccoli (page 56), we include two pounds of broccoli, stalks and all. Simplicity and economy go hand in hand, and it's truly gratifying to create a delicious meal following this philosophy.

Balancing Flavors
Salty, sweet, sour, and bitter (and the "fifth taste," umami) are flavors that our palates experience distinctly. A dish that balances them in harmony is a beautiful thing. Mezze Maniche with Guanciale, Chilies, and Ricotta (page 68) is a master class in balance: the sweet, creamy ricotta is set off by the rich pork and the hot chili flakes. When you're cooking up something of your own, look for this same sort of equilibrium. Does your dish need a bit of additional salt? Add a handful of capers, olives, or some anchovies as a more complex seasoning agent. Does the dish need

a bit more brightness? Give it a good squeeze of fresh lemon juice. Does it need a bit more texture? A generous showering of homemade bread crumbs should do the trick.

EQUIPMENT

Most of the equipment you'll need to make the recipes in this book may already be in your kitchen. We love making pasta dishes in a very large (14-inch) skillet, and we're sure you'll use it elsewhere too. A food processor and a KitchenAid mixer will come in handy. If you are in the market for some new kitchen equipment, do treat yourself to high-quality wares. Cooking and eating is something you'll be doing for the rest of your life, so you're investing in your future by buying equipment that will last. The equipment listed below should keep you primed to cook any of the recipes you'll find here.

- Kitchen scale
- Whisk
- 14-inch skillet or Dutch oven (for pasta dishes)
- Pasta pot
- Colander
- Tongs
- Chef's knife, paring knife
- Cutting board
- Rimmed baking sheets (aka sheet pans)
- Mortar and pestle
- Mixing bowls (stainless steel ones are lightweight, heatproof, and sturdy)
- Citrus rasp (Microplanes are the best)

Bucatini with Ramps

There's always a bit of a frenzy when ramps start showing up at the greenmarkets in spring. After a long, cold winter, it's a treat to bite into something fresh, sharp, and green-tasting, and ramps are some of the first alliums to sprout after the thaw. These leafy wild members of the lily family are a cause for celebration, heralding the real end of winter.

Make this dish with the first ramps of the season—slim, pencil-thin ones. The younger the ramp, the sweeter it is. And when you have tender young ramps, you can separate the tops from the bottoms and use the bulbs whole and unsliced. (As ramps mature and grow, they get bigger, thicker, and tougher, making slicing a necessity; see Note.) Plus, the long, lean shape of a young ramp echoes that of the bucatini, making for a really beautiful presentation full of silky textures. | **SERVES 4**

6 ounces young ramps,
⅛ to ¼ inch thick, ends
trimmed
6 tablespoons unsalted butter
Kosher salt
½ teaspoon chili flakes

1 pound bucatini
¼ cup finely grated Parmigiano-
Reggiano
About 3 tablespoons finely
grated Pecorino Romano, plus
more if desired

Rinse the ramps under cold running water to remove any grit and dry them well on paper towels. Separate the leaves from the bulbs. Cut the dark green leaves into 3-inch pieces and leave the bulbs whole.

In a very large skillet (or a Dutch oven; see page 37 for tips), melt the butter over high heat. Add the ramp bulbs and cook until golden, 2 to 3 minutes. Season with a large pinch of salt and the chili flakes. Add the ramp greens and toss until wilted, about 1 minute. Add 2 tablespoons water to the pan. Remove from the heat.

In a large pot of well-salted boiling water, cook the pasta according to the package instructions until 2 minutes shy of al dente; drain.

Toss the bucatini into the skillet with the ramps, along with the Parmigiano-Reggiano. Cook over medium heat until the pasta is al dente, 1 to 2 minutes, adding more water if the sauce seems dry.

Divide the pasta among four individual serving plates or bowls and finish each with 2 teaspoons or more of Pecorino Romano.

Note: If your ramps are young and slender, you can cook them whole. If they are more mature, you will need to slice the bottoms into small disks and slice the green tops into quarters.

Mezze Maniche with Asparagus and Ricotta

This dish is all about the ricotta: it melts easily on the warm noodles, completely coating the mezze maniche—a short, substantial, tube-shaped pasta—to create an upscale mac-and-cheese. The result is a beautiful milky pasta sauce that's velvety and luscious and sets off the grassy sweet flavor of the asparagus. Don't skimp on the black pepper; a generous amount of kick cuts through the richness of the ricotta. | SERVES 4

2 pounds asparagus, trimmed
¼ cup extra-virgin olive oil, plus
  more for drizzling
½ teaspoon kosher salt, or
  more to taste
2½ tablespoons unsalted butter

1 pound mezze maniche
  (or penne or rigatoni)
½ teaspoon freshly cracked
  black pepper, or more to taste
½ cup fresh ricotta

Slice the asparagus lengthwise in half. Cut crosswise into 1½-inch pieces (you should have about 7 cups).

In a very large skillet (or a Dutch oven; see page 37 for tips), warm the olive oil over medium-high heat. Add the asparagus and salt and cook until the asparagus begins to turn golden, about 2 minutes. Add 1 tablespoon of the butter. Continue cooking until the asparagus is golden all over, about 2 minutes more. Add 2 tablespoons water to the pan. Remove from the heat.

In a large pot of well-salted boiling water, cook the pasta according to the package instructions until 2 minutes shy of al dente; drain.

Toss the mezze maniche into the skillet with the asparagus, the remaining 1 1/2 tablespoons butter, and the pepper. Cook over medium heat until the pasta is al dente, 1 to 2 minutes, adding more water if the sauce seems dry. Taste and adjust the seasonings if necessary.

Divide the pasta among four individual serving plates or bowls and finish each with ricotta and a drizzle of olive oil.

Note: You have to use freshly ground pepper here if you want the dish to have a spicy-hot flavor. Pre-ground pepper doesn't really taste like much. When a recipe calls for a lot of black pepper for seasoning, taste as you go. Depending on the quality of the pepper and where it was grown, you might need to use more or less.

Spaghetti with Artichokes

The flavors in this recipe are very Roman: a combination of artichokes and Pecorino Romano, along with chili, garlic, and parsley, is something you'd see in a trattoria in the Eternal City. We like the addition of the softer Parmigiano-Reggiano, which imparts a milky creaminess to balance out the Pecorino's piquant saltiness. | **SERVES 4**

Juice of 2 lemons

8 small or 4 large artichokes

¾ cup extra-virgin olive oil, plus more for drizzling

8 garlic cloves, smashed and peeled

2 teaspoons kosher salt

½ teaspoon chili flakes

½ cup water

1 pound spaghetti

½ cup chopped flat-leaf parsley

3 tablespoons finely grated Parmigiano-Reggiano

1 tablespoon unsalted butter

¼ teaspoon freshly cracked black pepper

4 teaspoons finely grated Pecorino Romano, plus more if desired

To make the artichokes: Fill a large bowl with cold water and add the lemon juice. As you trim the artichokes, dip them occasionally into the lemon water to prevent browning.

Pull off and discard the outer leaves of each artichoke until you reach the pale green leaves at the center. Using a paring knife, trim away the dark green skin from the base. Slice off the very tip of the stem: you will see a pale green core in the stem, surrounded by a layer of darker green; use a paring knife to trim away as much of the dark green layer as possible; the white part of the stem is as tasty as the heart. Slice off the top third of the artichoke at the place where the dark green tops fade to pale green. Using a teaspoon (a serrated grapefruit spoon is perfect for this task), scoop out the hairy choke in the center of the artichoke, pulling out any pointed purple leaves with your fingers as well. The center of the artichoke should be completely clean. Drop the artichoke into the lemon water.

Halve the artichokes lengthwise, then slice lengthwise into ¼-inch-thick slices.

In a very large skillet (or a Dutch oven; see page 37 for tips), warm the olive oil over medium-high heat. Add the artichokes, garlic, and salt and cook until the artichokes are nicely browned and a little soft and the garlic is golden around the edges, 6 to 7 minutes. Add the chili flakes and cook for 1 minute. Add the ½ cup water (just enough to not quite cover the artichokes) and let simmer until the artichokes are very soft, about 2 minutes. There should still be some liquid remaining in the pan. Remove from the heat.

Meanwhile, in a large pot of well-salted boiling water, cook the pasta according to the package instructions until 2 minutes shy of al dente; drain.

Toss the spaghetti into the skillet with the artichokes, along with the parsley, Parmigiano-Reggiano, butter, and pepper, and cook until the pasta is just al dente, 1 to 2 minutes, adding 2 tablespoons water if the sauce seems dry.

Divide the pasta among four individual serving plates or bowls and finish each with a drizzle of olive oil and a teaspoon or more of Pecorino Romano.

Maccheroni with Pork Sausage and Broccoli Rabe

Broccoli rabe and sausage is a classic Italian combination you've probably seen hundreds of times—with good reason: the bitter, spicy greens make a pitch-perfect companion to rich, fatty sausage. Here the chewy, toothsome pasta adds a nice neutral element, breaking up the intensity of the sausage and greens. | SERVES 4

¼ cup extra-virgin olive oil
10 ounces Pork Sausage (recipe follows), **formed into 4 equal patties**
4 garlic cloves, smashed and peeled
½ teaspoon chili flakes
1 bunch broccoli rabe, trimmed and cut into bite-sized pieces (4 cups)

1 pound maccheroni
1 tablespoon unsalted butter
3 tablespoons finely grated Parmigiano-Reggiano, plus more for serving
½ teaspoon freshly cracked black pepper
Kosher salt

In a very large skillet (or a Dutch oven; see page 37 for tips), warm the olive oil over medium-high heat. Add the sausage patties and brown on both sides, 4 to 6 minutes total. Break up the meat with a spoon (the inside will still be pink and undercooked). Add the garlic and cook until golden, about 2 minutes. Add the chili flakes and cook until fragrant, about 30 seconds. Toss in the broccoli rabe and cook until wilted and tender, about 5 minutes. Add 2 tablespoons water to the pan. Remove from the heat.

In a large pot of well-salted boiling water, cook the pasta according to the package instructions until 2 minutes shy of al dente; drain.

CONTINUED

Toss the maccheroni into the skillet with the sausage and broccoli rabe mixture. Cook over medium heat for 1 minute, then add the butter and cook until the pasta is al dente, 1 to 2 minutes, adding more water if the sauce seems dry. Stir in the Parmigiano-Reggiano and pepper and cook for another 30 seconds. Season to taste with salt.

Divide the pasta among four individual serving plates or bowls and finish each with a generous sprinkle of cheese.

Pork Sausage

Making this sausage is a breeze—no stuffing involved. Brown it and toss it into this maccheroni recipe, where the little bites of crisp pork contrast with the bitter greens. Store it in ½-pound packages in the freezer and pull it out when the sausage urge strikes. | **MAKES ABOUT 2 POUNDS**

1¾ pounds ground pork shoulder, chilled
4 ounces ground pork belly, chilled
¾ teaspoon sugar

4 teaspoons kosher salt
1½ teaspoons cracked black pepper
¼ cup ice water

In a large bowl, combine all the ingredients. Using your hands (wear gloves, if you like), fold and mix together until all the ingredients are well distributed and the meat and fat bind together. When the mixture becomes noticeably stiff and sticky and starts to leave a greasy film on the sides of the bowl, stop mixing. Undermixing can lead to a dry, crumbly texture and overmixing can lead to tough, rubbery sausages. The mixture can be stored, well wrapped, for up to 5 days in the refrigerator or frozen for up to 6 months.

Penne with Zucchini and Mint

With its dense, firm texture that can withstand high cooking temperatures, Romanesco zucchini works really well in this early summer pasta dish. Unlike the usual zucchini, it can actually pick up some caramelized brown color in the pan without falling apart. Zucchini tends to be a mild-tasting vegetable, so browning it deeply is important for the flavor here.

To add some body to this otherwise delicate dish, Andrew uses a combination of butter and olive oil—the butter adds richness and helps to emulsify the sauce, and the oil contributes a floral note and a slight bite. Mint and zucchini are a classic Italian combination, and this delicious pasta will show you why. | **SERVES 4**

1¾ pounds zucchini, preferably Romanesco, trimmed
¼ cup extra-virgin olive oil, plus more for drizzling
Kosher salt
1 pound penne
4 tablespoons unsalted butter
8 garlic cloves, smashed and peeled

¼ cup plus a scant 3 tablespoons finely grated Parmigiano-Reggiano, plus more if desired
3 tablespoons chopped mint
¼ teaspoon freshly cracked black pepper

Slice each zucchini into 2-inch-by-¼-inch batons (you will have about 5 cups).

In a very large skillet (or a Dutch oven; see page 37 for tips), warm 2 tablespoons of the olive oil over high heat. Add half the zucchini, season with salt, and cook, without moving it, until dark golden and almost tender, 2 to 3 minutes. With a slotted spoon, transfer the zucchini to a paper-towel-lined plate. Add another 2 tablespoons olive oil to the skillet and repeat with the remaining zucchini. Add 2 tablespoons water to the pan. Remove from the heat.

In a large pot of well-salted boiling water, cook the pasta according to the package instructions until 2 minutes shy of al dente; drain.

In the same skillet, melt 3 tablespoons of the butter over medium heat. Add the garlic and cook for 2 to 3 minutes. Toss in the penne and zucchini, and cook until the pasta is al dente, 1 to 2 minutes, adding more water if the sauce seems dry. Toss in the ¼ cup Parmigiano-Reggiano and the remaining tablespoon of butter. Add the mint and season to taste with salt and the pepper.

Divide the pasta among four individual serving plates or bowls and finish each with a drizzle of olive oil and 2 teaspoons or more of the cheese.

Spaghetti with Herbs and Ricotta

When fresh herbs finally arrive at the farmers' market in the early summer, we rush home with fragrant bundles to make this creamy, light spaghetti. The ricotta acts as a vehicle for all the lovely herbs, allowing them to cling to the pasta without making the dish heavy. This recipe calls for leafy, soft herbs—parsley, mint, and basil; woody, intensely flavored herbs such as rosemary or thyme would overpower the delicacy and sweetness of the cheese. If you're lucky enough to have some earth or a window box in which to plant an annual herb garden, this is a brilliant way to make use of that sudden surplus that seems to happen all at once. | **SERVES 4**

½ cup extra-virgin olive oil, plus more for drizzling

4 garlic cloves, smashed and peeled

½ teaspoon chili flakes

1 pound spaghetti

½ cup fresh ricotta

Kosher salt

¼ teaspoon freshly cracked black pepper, plus more to taste

1 tablespoon unsalted butter

½ cup coarsely chopped flat-leaf parsley

¼ cup coarsely chopped basil

¼ cup coarsely chopped mint

¼ cup coarsely grated Parmigiano-Reggiano, plus more if desired

In a very large skillet (or a Dutch oven; see page 37 for tips), warm the olive oil over medium-high heat. Add the garlic and cook until fragrant and light golden, about 3 minutes. Add the chili flakes and cook for 30 seconds more. Add 2 tablespoons water to the pan. Remove from the heat.

CONTINUED

In a large pot of well-salted boiling water, cook the pasta according to the package instructions until 2 minutes shy of al dente; drain and reserve a cup or two of the pasta water.

Season the ricotta with salt and pepper.

Toss the spaghetti into the skillet with the garlic, along with the butter and pepper. Cook over medium heat until the pasta is just al dente, 1 to 2 minutes. Then add the ricotta, herbs, and Parmigiano-Reggiano to the pasta and toss with tongs until the ricotta loosely coats the spaghetti, adding more pasta water as needed to smooth out the texture.

Divide the pasta among four individual serving plates or bowls. Finish each with a drizzle of olive oil and more Parmigiano-Reggiano, if desired.

Spaghettini with Shrimp

This is a very nontraditional way to make pasta, borrowing on the French technique of using stock as a foundation for sauce. In Italy, you don't normally see pasta prepared with stock, but here it works to intensify the delicate flavor of sweet, fresh shrimp. This recipe takes longer to make than most others in this book, but the process is fairly straightforward. For the stock, whole shrimp are peeled, the shells separated from the meat, and the shells and heads are toasted to bring out their flavor and add a layer of caramelization to the sauce. Then the pan is deglazed with a dash of white vermouth, which imparts a lovely herbal quality and complexity.

Once you have the stock, the rest of the dish is utterly simple: reduce the stock with a little garlic and pinch of chili, then brown the shrimp. Delicate spaghettini tangles around the golden-edged shrimp, and a finish of scallions and lemon adds a sunny brilliance. | **SERVES 4**

¼ cup extra-virgin olive oil, plus
  more for drizzling
1½ pounds large shrimp, peeled
  and deveined
Kosher salt
3 tablespoons unsalted butter
4 garlic cloves, smashed
  and peeled

½ teaspoon chili flakes
4 cups Shrimp Stock
  (recipe follows)
1 pound spaghettini
½ cup thinly sliced scallions
Juice of 1 lemon, or to taste
½ teaspoon freshly cracked
  black pepper

In a very large skillet (or a Dutch oven; see page 37 for tips), warm ¼ cup of the olive oil over medium-high heat. Season the shrimp with salt. Once the oil is hot and shimmering, add the shrimp (cook in batches if necessary) and sear, without moving it, until the undersides are brown. Transfer the shrimp to a bowl. (If you cook the shrimp on both sides, it will overcook when added to the pasta.)

Return the skillet to the heat and add 1 tablespoon of the butter, the garlic, and the chili flakes and cook until the garlic is fragrant and golden, about 2 minutes. Pour in the shrimp stock, bring to a simmer, and simmer until reduced by half, 10 to 15 minutes.

While the sauce reduces, bring a large pot of well-salted water to a boil. Cook the pasta according to the package instructions until 2 minutes shy of al dente; drain.

Toss the spaghettini into the skillet with the reduced stock, along with the scallions. Cook over medium heat until the pasta is al dente, 1 to 2 minutes. Toss in the shrimp, the remaining 2 tablespoons butter, the lemon juice, and the pepper, and stir to combine and heat through.

Divide the pasta among four individual serving plates or bowls and finish each with a drizzle of olive oil.

Note: While you could use purchased shrimp stock for this recipe, it might not have the same depth of flavor as the homemade. And this is such a bare-bones dish, it pays to take the time to make your own stock. (Plus, prepared shrimp stock can be hard to find.)

Shrimp Stock

5 tablespoons extra-virgin
  olive oil
1¼ pounds shrimp shells
  and heads
3 tablespoons dry vermouth
2 onions, coarsely chopped
3 celery stalks, coarsely
  chopped

8 garlic cloves, coarsely
  chopped
⅓ cup chopped flat-leaf parsley
1½ teaspoons fennel seeds
1 bay leaf
1 dried chili
1½ teaspoons tomato paste
8 cups water

In a large pot, warm 1½ tablespoons of the olive oil over medium-high heat. Add half the shrimp shells and heads and sear them, stirring, until fragrant and golden in places, about 5 minutes. Transfer to a bowl. Repeat with 1½ tablespoons more olive oil and the remaining shells and heads. Before removing the second batch of shells, pour the vermouth into the pot and deglaze, scraping the bottom of the pot. Transfer the shells to the bowl.

Add the remaining 2 tablespoons olive oil to the pot. Stir in the onions, celery, garlic, parsley, fennel seeds, bay leaf, and chili and cook over medium heat, stirring occasionally, until the vegetables are soft and translucent, about 10 minutes. Stir in the tomato paste and increase the heat to medium-high. Cook, stirring occasionally, until the tomato paste browns a bit.

Return the shrimp shells and heads to the pot, pour in the water, and bring to a simmer. Cook for 1 hour. Strain the stock through a fine-mesh sieve, pressing on the solids with the back of a spoon to extract the flavor. Let cool. The stock will keep, in an airtight container, in the refrigerator for 1 week or in the freezer for 3 months.

Pasta Techniques

1. There's an art and a science to matching pasta shape to sauce. Sauces that are fairly fluid and smooth, such as the one in Linguine with Meyer Lemon (page 82), are lovely paired with long pastas like linguine, spaghetti, or bucatini; the sauce will drape and wrap the noodles.

2. When there's a lot of stuff or bits in the sauce (see Maccheroni with Pork Sausage and Broccoli Rabe, page 23), short pastas have the necessary nooks and crannies to give all the elements of a chunkier sauce a place to congregate. Large tubular pastas, such as rigatoni and paccheri, have wide holes that can capture the big chunks of a meat ragu, whole beans, or bite-sized pieces of seafood. So, when picking your pasta size and shape, think about the texture of your sauce and pair them accordingly.

3. Always make sure your pasta cooking water is adequately salted. Most Americans add a pinch of salt to the pot, but pasta needs a generous amount of salt in the water to bring out its wheaty flavor. The water should taste markedly salty, like the ocean—use about 1/3 cup kosher salt per large pot of water (and don't worry; most of the salt ends up going down the drain with the pasta water). As the pasta cooks, it absorbs salt and becomes seasoned through and through.

4. The best pan for simmering pasta and sauce together is a wide deep skillet or sauté pan. A 14-inch pan may seem enormous, but it's actually ideal for sauce and pasta to feed 4 to 6 people (about a pound of noodles). The recipes in this book are written for this amount. However, if you halve everything to feed 2 or 3, a 10- or 12-inch skillet will work fine.

5. Another option is to use a Dutch oven. Dutch ovens have higher sides than skillets, making it harder to evaporate liquid. They also retain heat beautifully—which is good for braises but not for pasta, as too much residual heat in the pot can wilt the noodles. If using a Dutch oven, make sure the sauce is cooked down until it's thick before you add the pasta, then go light when adding water to the pan. As soon as the pasta is ready, serve it or transfer it to a warmed serving platter. You don't want it to sit in the hot pot and continue to cook.

6. After the pasta is added to the pan with the sauce, let it cook until the pasta absorbs the flavor of the sauce, 1 to 3 minutes. If the pan looks dry, you can add a little plain water. Don't use the pasta cooking water here; it could make the sauce too salty.

Bucatini Fra Diavolo

A gutsy, punchy "red sauce" pasta is just right for the beginning of summer—here the Pecorino Romano lends a salty bite, and the spicy chili flakes add a sharp kick that is especially welcome when the weather starts to warm. We make this dish just before fresh tomatoes start showing up at the market but while bunches of herbs are available in abundance.

Don't imagine this as the *fra diavolo* (Italian for "brother devil," because of the fiery seasoning) you might remember from Italian restaurant menus in the '80s. This recipe was inspired by one in Fred Plotkin's *The Authentic Pasta Book*. Aside from the aroma of the fresh herbs, the secret to this sauce is a copious hit of olive oil. It adds a fruity richness that plays beautifully off the chili and tomatoes. | **SERVES 4**

¾ cup extra-virgin olive oil, plus more for drizzling

8 garlic cloves, smashed and peeled

1 teaspoon chili flakes

2 cups San Marzano tomato puree

Kosher salt

1 pound bucatini

¼ cup finely chopped basil

¼ cup finely chopped mint

¼ cup finely chopped flat-leaf parsley

1 tablespoon unsalted butter

3 tablespoons finely grated Parmigiano-Reggiano

¼ teaspoon freshly cracked black pepper

Scant 3 tablespoons finely grated Pecorino Romano, plus more if desired

In a very large skillet (or a Dutch oven; see page 37 for tips), warm the olive oil over medium-high heat. Add the garlic and cook until fragrant and golden, about 3 minutes. Add the chili flakes and cook

for 30 seconds more. Add the tomato puree, season with salt to taste, and cook until the oil separates, the tomato solids start to fry, and the sauce has thickened, 10 to 12 minutes. Add 2 tablespoons water to the pan. Remove from the heat.

In a large pot of well-salted boiling water, cook the pasta according to the package instructions until 2 minutes shy of al dente; drain.

Toss the bucatini into the skillet with the tomato sauce, herbs, and butter. Cook over medium heat until the pasta is just al dente, 1 to 2 minutes. Stir in the Parmigiano-Reggiano and pepper, adding more water if the sauce seems dry.

Divide the pasta among four individual serving plates or bowls and finish each with 2 teaspoons or more of Pecorino Romano and a drizzle of olive oil.

Bucatini alla Puttanesca

If you love to make Italian food at home, you probably have
all these ingredients in your pantry or refrigerator at this very
moment. While this dish is bursting with savory flavors, the
translation of *puttanesca* is rather unsavory. Let's just say that
this classic Italian preparation is named after the ladies of the
night who, when arriving home in the wee hours, could whip up
a satisfying meal using ingredients they had on hand. If you can
find canned Italian cherry tomatoes, use them. The sweetness of
cherry tomatoes is most welcome against the salty, briny flavors
of the capers, olives, and anchovies (though you could substitute
canned diced tomatoes). When you're craving a bowl of pasta
swimming in big, bold flavors, this puttanesca more than fits
the bill. | **SERVES 4**

¼ cup extra virgin olive oil, plus
   more for drizzling
4 large cloves garlic, smashed
   and peeled
4 tablespoons unsalted butter
9 anchovy fillets
½ teaspoon chili flakes
1 teaspoon dried oregano
2 cups canned Italian cherry
   tomatoes or canned diced
   tomatoes, drained

3 tablespoons salt-packed
   capers, soaked, rinsed, and
   drained (see Note)
1 pound bucatini
½ cup **Nocellara or Cerignola
   olives**, pitted and chopped
½ cup chopped flat-leaf parsley
Kosher salt and freshly cracked
   black pepper

In a very large skillet (or a Dutch oven; see page 37 for tips),
warm the olive oil over medium-high heat. Add the garlic and cook
until golden brown, about 1 minute. Add the butter, anchovies,

chili flakes, and oregano and cook for 2 minutes, breaking up the anchovy fillets with the back of a large spoon until they dissolve. Add the tomatoes and capers and cook, breaking up the tomatoes, until much of the liquid has evaporated and the oil has separated out and puddled on the sauce's surface, about 10 minutes. Remove from the heat.

In a large pot of well-salted boiling water, cook the pasta according to the package instructions until 2 minutes shy of al dente; drain.

Toss the bucatini into the skillet with the tomato mixture along with the olives and parsley. Cook over medium heat until the pasta is al dente, 1 to 2 minutes, adding a few tablespoons of water if the sauce seems dry. Season to taste with salt and pepper.

Divide the pasta among four individual serving plates or bowls and finish each with a drizzle of olive oil.

Note: We use capers from Pantelleria (see Resources, page 89), which are among the best available. They come packed in salt, so you need to rinse and then soak them before using.

Put them in a bowl, cover them with a lot of cold water, and let them soak for 3 to 5 hours, changing the water two or three times. In the end, they should taste seasoned but not overly salty. Once they are soaked, spread the capers on a clean cloth and let them dry out for a few hours. Then store them in a tightly covered container in the fridge for a week or two.

Linguine with Tomatoes, Basil, and Parmigiano-Reggiano

Here's a fantastic dish to make at the height of tomato season. We especially love to use Ramapo tomatoes, which while technically not heirloom tomatoes have the flavor of them. The hybrid was originally developed at Rutgers University in 1968, and we think it is one of the finest beefsteak tomatoes in existence. Ramapo tomatoes are intensely red and have an intoxicating perfume. When genuinely ripe, they are very soft, very juicy, and deeply sweet. Their skin is more delicate than that of conventional tomatoes, making them a great choice for this dish—you don't get any tough, unappealing curls of skin accumulating in your sauce. After you bring the tomatoes home from the market, let them sit on your counter for 2 to 4 days— you'll be rewarded with absurdly ripe, concentrated tomato flavor. The sweetness will remind you that a tomato is botanically a fruit. Unfortunately, many farms stopped growing those tomatoes because they are fragile and don't travel well. If you can't get them, use the best, ripest tomatoes you can get.

Once you've got ripe tomatoes, this sauce comes together quickly. There's no need to develop any flavors, since the tomatoes are full of flavor already. You want the fresh, vibrant essence of tomato to shine. Add a few torn basil leaves, and it's perfect—though an extra sprinkle of Parmigiano-Reggiano doesn't hurt. | **SERVES 4**

CONTINUED

½ cup extra-virgin olive oil, plus more for drizzling
4 garlic cloves, coarsely chopped
1¾ pounds ripe tomatoes, cored and chopped (about 5 cups)

1 pound linguine
1 tablespoon unsalted butter
12 basil leaves, torn
¼ cup finely grated Parmigiano-Reggiano, plus more for serving
Kosher salt

In a very large skillet (or a Dutch oven; see page 37 for tips), warm the olive oil over medium-high heat. Add the garlic and cook until fragrant, about 2 minutes. Add the tomatoes and cook for 5 minutes, until they start to break down and most of the liquid evaporates. Add 2 tablespoons water to the pan. Remove from the heat.

In a large pot of well-salted boiling water, cook the pasta according to the package instructions until 2 minutes shy of al dente; drain.

Toss the linguine into the skillet with the tomatoes, butter, and basil. Cook over medium heat until the pasta is just al dente, 1 to 2 minutes. Toss in the Parmigiano-Reggiano and season to taste with salt, adding more water if the sauce seems dry.

Divide the pasta among four individual serving plates or bowls and finish each with a drizzle of olive oil and a sprinkle of cheese.

Note: We're not fans of basil chiffonade—that is, finely slivered basil. The long strips seem overwrought, and all that contact with the knife basically just bruises the tender leaves. Instead, pull off the leaves from the basil branches and tear them into small pieces before adding them to the pasta; torn basil just tastes better!

Paccheri with Swordfish, Olives, Capers, and Mint

People often think of swordfish as a strong-flavored fish, but I think that's more about its texture, which is meaty and dense. The flesh is actually sweet and mild. And for this dish, swordfish's density is an advantage, allowing for lovely, resilient chunks that can stand up to the al dente pasta. Their size and texture go well with the pasta called *paccheri* (in Italian it means "a slap in the mouth")—the bits of fish nestle nicely inside the wide openings of the pasta—but you can also use rigatoni or any other large tubular shape. The pungency of chili flakes, mint, and fennel seeds make a nice contrast to the gentle saline flavor of the fish. | **SERVES 4 TO 6**

1½ pounds skinless swordfish steaks, cut into 1-inch-by-1-inch-by-½-inch chunks

Kosher salt and freshly cracked black pepper

½ cup extra-virgin olive oil, plus more for drizzling

3 tablespoons salt-packed capers, soaked, rinsed, and drained (see Note, page 43), or drained brined capers

¼ cup Nocellara or Cerignola olives, pitted and roughly chopped

4 teaspoons chopped garlic

1 teaspoon fennel seeds, preferably Sicilian (see Note)

1 teaspoon chili flakes

1 pound paccheri (see the headnote)

¼ cup chopped flat-leaf parsley

3 tablespoons chopped mint

Fresh lemon juice

Season the fish with salt and pepper. In a very large skillet (or a Dutch oven; see page 37 for tips), warm ¼ cup of the olive oil over high heat. Add the fish and cook, without moving, until browned on

one side, about 2 minutes. (Cook in batches if necessary to avoid overcrowding the pan.) Transfer the fish to a platter and set aside.

In the same skillet, warm the remaining ¼ cup olive oil over medium-high heat. Add the capers and fry until they start to brown, 1 to 2 minutes. Add the olives, garlic, fennel seeds, and chili flakes and cook until everything is toasty and fragrant, about 2 minutes. Add 2 tablespoons of water to the pan. Remove from the heat.

In a large pot of well-salted boiling water, cook the pasta according to the package instructions until 2 minutes shy of al dente; drain.

Toss the paccheri into the skillet with the caper mixture, along with the swordfish. Cook over medium heat until the pasta is al dente, 1 to 2 minutes, adding more water if the sauce seems dry. Stir in the parsley and mint and season with salt, pepper, and lemon juice.

Divide the pasta among four individual serving plates or bowls and finish each with a drizzle of olive oil.

Note: Here we use fennel seeds from Sicily—they are shorter, fatter, and more fragrant than the typical fennel seeds. You can get them at Manicaretti (see Resources, page 89).

Paccheri with Squid, Cherry Tomatoes, Peppers, and Capers

To do this dish justice, you need to cook the squid low and slow. During the braising process, a deeply flavored, sea-sweet broth develops, providing an ideal base for the sauce. If tomatoes and peppers aren't in season, experiment with other seasonal vegetables—fresh peas in the spring, or shell beans in early autumn. | **SERVES 4 TO 6**

1¼ pounds cleaned squid, tentacles and heads separated

½ cup plus 1 tablespoon extra-virgin olive oil, plus more for drizzling

Kosher salt

¼ cup salt-packed capers, soaked, rinsed, and drained (see Note, page 43)

2 cups (about 28) **cherry tomatoes**

¾ cup diced red bell pepper

2½ tablespoons chopped garlic

6 tablespoons finely chopped flat-leaf parsley

1 teaspoon chili flakes

1 cup dry white wine

1 pound paccheri or other pasta (see Note)

Rinse the squid under cool running water; drain. Pat dry with paper towels, then transfer to a plate.

Heat a very large skillet (or a Dutch oven; see page 37 for tips) over high heat until very hot, about 5 minutes. Add 2 tablespoons of the olive oil. Season the squid with salt, then add about half the squid to the pan and cook, without moving it, until browned on one side. Transfer to a plate. (Do not overcrowd the pan; if it doesn't hold half the squid comfortably, cook it in 3 instead of 2 batches, using 2 tablespoons oil for each batch.) Repeat with the remaining squid.

CONTINUED

Add 3 tablespoons olive oil to the pan and reduce the heat to medium-high. Add the capers and sauté until they begin to brown, 2 to 3 minutes. Transfer the capers to the plate with the squid. Add the remaining 2 tablespoons olive oil to the pan, stir in the tomatoes and bell pepper, and cook for 2 minutes. At this point the bottom of the pan should have a nice brown fond (the bits sticking to the bottom of the pan). Add the garlic, 2 tablespoons of the parsley, and the chili flakes and cook until the garlic is fragrant, about 2 minutes.

Return the squid and capers to the pan, pour in the white wine, and cook until the wine is reduced by half. Add ½ cup water, cover the pan, and simmer over low heat until the squid is tender, about 20 minutes.

While the squid simmers, in a large pot of well-salted boiling water, cook the pasta according to the package instructions until 2 minutes shy of al dente; drain.

When the squid is just tender, add the pasta to the pan and cook over medium heat, tossing well, until the pasta is al dente, 1 to 2 minutes. Add the remaining ¼ cup parsley and toss to combine. If the sauce seems dry, add a little water.

Divide the pasta among four individual serving plates or bowls and finish each with a drizzle of olive oil.

Note: If you can't find paccheri, look for calamarata, which is basically half a paccheri noodle, and works perfectly, since it's almost the same size as the length of the squid pieces. If you can't find either one, substitute spaghetti, bucatini, or even linguine.

Spaghetti with Chickpeas

It's not often that you see a starchy ingredient like chickpeas tossed in with pasta, but it's done beautifully in Italy, and this is actually a relatively light and nutritious dish. Because there's no cheese, the flavors maintain a discernible brightness. Browning and crisping the chickpeas in olive oil intensifies their nutty flavor. Once they go into the pan, resist the urge to move them around—let them sit and sizzle, soaking up the olive oil and turning golden and crunchy. The flavor of the chickpeas is heightened by the pungent notes of garlic and chili, and anchovy lends its classic savory saltiness. | **SERVES 4**

FOR THE CHICKPEAS
1 pound dried chickpeas
5 cups water
½ cup extra-virgin olive oil
2 tablespoons kosher salt
1 small onion (or ½ large), cut in half
3 large garlic cloves, smashed and peeled
1 bay leaf
1 small rosemary sprig

¾ cup olive oil
1 pound spaghetti
½ cup finely chopped flat-leaf parsley
¼ cup finely chopped mint
¼ teaspoon freshly cracked black pepper
Juice of ½ lemon
Kosher salt

To make the chickpeas: Soak the chickpeas in a bowl of cool water to cover for at least 8 hours, or up to overnight.

Drain the chickpeas and place in a large saucepan. Cover with the 5 cups water and add the ½ cup olive oil and the salt.

CONTINUED

Make a sachet by laying a triple layer of cheesecloth on a work surface. Place the onion, garlic, bay leaf, and rosemary in the center of the cheesecloth and tie the corners of the cheesecloth together to make a bundle. Place the sachet in the saucepan and bring to a boil over medium-high heat. Skim any foamy scum that comes to the surface. Reduce the heat to low to maintain a simmer, cover the pot, and cook the chickpeas until tender, 30 minutes to 1½ hours (depending on the freshness of the chickpeas). Taste regularly to check the tenderness. Drain the chickpeas.

In a very large skillet (or a Dutch oven; see page 37 for tips), warm ½ cup of the olive oil over high heat until shimmering. Add the chickpeas and fry, without stirring, until they are darkly colored on one side, 3 to 5 minutes. Add the remaining ¼ cup olive oil and the garlic cloves and cook until the garlic is fragrant and light golden, about 2 minutes. Add the anchovies and cook, stirring and mashing, until they dissolve. Add the chili flakes and cook for 30 seconds. Add 2 tablespoons water to the pan. Remove from the heat.

In a large pot of well-salted boiling water, cook the pasta according to the package instructions until 2 minutes shy of al dente; drain.

Toss the spaghetti into the skillet with the chickpeas, herbs, and pepper. Cook, tossing, until the pasta is al dente, 1 to 2 minutes, adding more water if the sauce seems dry. Add the lemon juice and season with salt to taste.

Divide the pasta among four individual serving plates or bowls and finish each with a drizzle of olive oil.

Note: People don't often think of adding lemon juice to pasta, but it's a great complement to pastas that are on the richer, starchier side. It can really transform a dish, contributing brightness and complexity.

Penne with Broccoli

We usually make this dish in the late summer and early fall, when the best local broccoli is available at our farmers' market. Supermarket broccoli stems can be bland and woody, but at the farmers' market, the entire stalk (florets, leaves, stems) is flavorful and tender. With good seasonal broccoli, there's no need to limit yourself to florets—cook it all; it's delicious.

Since broccoli is a pretty powerful-tasting vegetable, it can stand up to a good amount of garlic and chili: two sweet, pungent cloves of garlic per person isn't overdoing it here. And be diligent when it comes to browning the broccoli. In this recipe, the browning is almost an ingredient in itself, providing a solid flavor foundation for all the other elements of the dish. | **SERVES 4**

7 tablespoons extra-virgin olive oil, plus more for drizzling

8 cups 1-inch broccoli florets and peeled tender stems (see Notes) (from about 2 pounds broccoli)

1 teaspoon kosher salt

8 garlic cloves, crushed and peeled

½ teaspoon chili flakes

1 pound penne

1 tablespoon unsalted butter

¼ teaspoon freshly cracked black pepper

3 tablespoons finely grated Parmigiano-Reggiano

4 teaspoons finely grated Pecorino Romano, plus more if desired

In a very large skillet (or a Dutch oven; see page 37 for tips), warm 3 tablespoons of the olive oil over medium-high heat. Add the broccoli and ½ teaspoon of the salt. Once the broccoli has

absorbed the olive oil, add the remaining ¼ cup oil, increase the heat to high, and let the broccoli get very brown and tender, about 7 minutes. Add the garlic and chili flakes and cook until fragrant, about 30 seconds. Add 2 tablespoons water to the pan. Remove from the heat.

In a large pot of well-salted boiling water, cook the pasta according to the package instructions until 2 minutes shy of al dente; drain.

Toss the penne into the skillet with the broccoli, butter, and pepper. Cook over medium heat until the pasta is al dente, 1 to 2 minutes, adding more water if the sauce seems dry. Stir in the Parmigiano-Reggiano and season with the remaining ½ teaspoon salt.

Divide the pasta among four individual serving plates or bowls and finish each with 1 teaspoon Pecorino Romano. Drizzle with olive oil and sprinkle with additional Pecorino, if desired.

Notes: Depending on how you cut your broccoli, you could also use mezze maniche, rigatoni, or maccheroni here. Just make sure to cut the broccoli to approximate the pasta's size and shape to make this dish work best.

If you want to use whole broccoli stalks here instead of just the florets, peel the stems and cut them into pieces the same size as the florets (and the pasta), and cook them along with the florets. You can toss in the leaves too—they have great flavor.

Fusilli with Black Kale Pesto

This pesto dish calls for kale in place of handfuls of perfumed basil leaves, making for an altogether quieter, softer, and warmer pasta. With the toothy, satisfying chunks of walnuts and the Parmigiano-Reggiano, fusilli works well for this dish—all those curves and crevices are a great vehicle for the sauce. Kale is one of those hardy greens you can find all winter long, and this is an out-of-the-ordinary way to use it. In the dead of winter, treat yourself to this bright-tasting dish, bursting with green freshness and fragrant lemon zest. | **SERVES 4**

½ cup plus 2 tablespoons
   walnuts
½ cup plus ¾ teaspoon kosher
   salt, or more to taste
12 ounces (about 1 bunch) **Tuscan
   kale, center ribs removed**
¾ cup extra-virgin olive oil, plus
   more for drizzling

8 garlic cloves, thinly sliced
Finely grated zest of 1 lemon
1 pound fusilli
¼ cup finely grated Parmigiano-
   Reggiano, plus more if
   desired

Preheat the oven to 350°F. Spread the walnuts on a rimmed baking sheet. Toast until golden and fragrant, 7 to 10 minutes. Set aside.

In a large pot, bring 4 quarts water and the ½ cup of salt to a boil. Prepare a bowl of ice water. Add the kale leaves to the pot and cook until tender, 2 to 3 minutes. Using tongs, immediately transfer the kale to the ice water to cool. Drain, squeeze the excess water from the greens, and transfer to a plate (it's okay if they retain a bit of water, as long as they aren't dripping).

CONTINUED

In a very large skillet (or a Dutch oven; see page 37 for tips), warm ¼ cup of the olive oil over medium-low heat. Add the garlic and cook until tender but not browned, about 2 minutes. Add 2 tablespoons water to the pan. Remove from the heat.

In a food processor, combine the walnuts, kale, garlic-oil mixture, the remaining ½ cup olive oil, the remaining ¾ teaspoon salt, and the lemon zest. Pulse until the mixture forms a coarse paste, then transfer the pesto to the large skillet.

In a large pot of well-salted boiling water, cook the pasta according to the package instructions until 2 minutes shy of al dente; drain.

Toss the fusilli into the skillet with the pesto. Cook over medium heat until the pasta is al dente, 1 to 2 minutes, adding more water if the sauce seems dry. Taste and add more salt if needed.

Divide the pasta among four individual serving plates or bowls and finish each with a tablespoon or more of Parmigiano-Reggiano and a drizzle of olive oil.

Penne with Spicy Cauliflower

The secret to deeply flavored cauliflower is cooking it until it's good and caramelized all over; the darker it gets, the richer it will taste.

One thing to keep in mind: cauliflower releases more water than broccoli, meaning it takes longer to brown, so make sure to get the pan piping hot before adding it. Cooked cauliflower has a pleasant soft texture, and here the garnish of crisp bread crumbs provides a lovely contrast. The bread crumbs for this dish are bigger than usual, like a cross between a crumb and a crouton, with loads of texture and crunch. Don't try to substitute store-bought bread crumbs; they won't have the same effect. | **SERVES 4**

⅓ cup 1-inch pieces country-style bread

⅔ cup plus 2 teaspoons extra-virgin olive oil, plus more for drizzling

1 large head cauliflower, trimmed and cored

8 garlic cloves, coarsely chopped

Kosher salt

1 pound penne

2½ tablespoons unsalted butter

2 teaspoons chili flakes

¼ cup finely grated Parmigiano-Reggiano

Freshly cracked black pepper

3 tablespoons finely grated Pecorino Romano, plus more if desired

Preheat the oven to 300°F. In a large bowl, toss the bread pieces with the 2 teaspoons olive oil. Spread them out on a baking sheet and toast until they are dry, about 10 minutes. Increase the heat to 400°F and toast until the bread is dark golden brown, about 10 minutes more.

CONTINUED

Crumble the croutons into small pieces or pulse very coarsely in a food processor; you want them to still have some texture.

Cut the cauliflower into pieces about twice the size of a penne noodle.

In a very large skillet (or a Dutch oven; see page 37 for tips), warm ⅓ cup of the olive oil over medium-high heat. Add half the cauliflower and cook until it is well browned, about 5 minutes. Add half the garlic and cook for 30 seconds. Season with salt and transfer to a bowl. Repeat with the remaining ⅓ cup olive oil, cauliflower, and garlic. Season with salt and add to the bowl. Set the pan aside.

In a large pot of well-salted boiling water, cook the pasta according to the package instructions until 2 minutes shy of al dente; drain.

Return all of the cauliflower to the skillet, add 1 tablespoon of the butter and the chili flakes, and cook over medium heat for 30 seconds. Add 2 tablespoons water and a large pinch of salt and simmer until the cauliflower is tender, 2 to 3 minutes.

Add the penne to the skillet, along with the remaining 1½ tablespoons butter and the Parmigiano-Reggiano. Toss until a nice emulsified sauce forms and the pasta is al dente, 1 to 2 minutes, adding more water if the sauce seems dry. Season generously with pepper, then remove from the heat and toss in the bread crumbs and Pecorino Romano; toss again.

Divide the pasta among four individual serving plates or bowls and finish each with a drizzle of olive oil and more Pecorino, if desired.

Note: If you get cauliflower from the farmers' market, be sure to use the chopped leaves—they are sweet and mild and will add a great deal of flavor and texture to the dish.

Penne with Cabbage and Provolone Piccante

This hearty pasta was inspired by a Northern Italian dish from Val d'Aosta made with cabbage and Fontina. We use provolone instead of Fontina. It's still soft and moist enough to create a creamy sauce that coats the noodles and cabbage, but its slightly sharp finish adds some complexity to the mix. This is a great dish to turn to in the winter when you want something warm and indulgent. | SERVES 4

½ cup extra virgin olive oil, plus more for drizzling

One 2-pound green cabbage, cored and cut into 1-inch squares (about 9 cups)

4 large garlic cloves, crushed and peeled

Kosher salt

4 tablespoons unsalted butter

½ teaspoon chili flakes

1 pound penne

½ cup plus 2 tablespoons grated provolone piccante, plus more if desired

Freshly cracked black pepper

In a very large skillet (or a Dutch oven; see page 37 for tips), warm the olive oil over medium-high heat. Add the cabbage and cook, stirring often, until it turns golden, 7 to 8 minutes. Add the garlic, a pinch of salt, 2 tablespoons of the butter, and the chili flakes. Cook until the garlic is light golden and fragrant, 2 to 3 minutes. Add 2 tablespoons water to the pan. Remove from the heat.

In a large pot of well-salted boiling water, cook the pasta according to the package instructions until 2 minutes shy of al dente; drain.

Toss the penne into the skillet with the cabbage and the remaining 2 tablespoons butter. Cook over medium heat until the pasta is al

dente, 1 to 2 minutes, adding a little more water if the sauce seems dry. Add ½ cup of the provolone and black pepper to taste.

Divide the pasta among four individual serving plates or bowls and finish each with ½ tablespoon or more cheese and a drizzle of olive oil.

Note: This is a recipe made for regular green cabbage. Red cabbage is too sweet, and the color isn't right for the dish. Savoy cabbage could work as well.

Mezze Maniche with Guanciale, Chilies, and Ricotta

This is our version of *alla gricia* (a classic Roman dish) made with guanciale—rich, cured hog jowl. The star of the show here is the guanciale. There is some well-made commercially available guanciale, but it can be hard to find, so feel free to substitute pancetta (or even bacon). Pancetta has less fat and is less gamey than guanciale, but it will still be delicious in its own, milder way. A sprinkle of chili is toasted in the rendered guanciale fat, yielding a nice prickle of heat. Tossing ricotta in at the end creates a lush and creamy sauce, with a mildness that softens some of the more rustic aspects of the guanciale. This has all the best elements of a classic *alla gricia*, but the sharp corners have been rounded off for a more elegant dish. | **SERVES 4**

12 ounces guanciale,
  pancetta, or bacon, diced
  (generous 2 cups)
¼ teaspoon chili flakes
1 pound mezze maniche
  (or penne or rigatoni)

2 tablespoons unsalted butter
1 tablespoon plus 4 teaspoons
  finely grated Pecorino
  Romano, plus more if desired
½ cup fresh ricotta
Extra-virgin olive oil

Heat a very large skillet (or a Dutch oven; see page 37 for tips) over medium-high heat. Add the guanciale and cook, stirring, until it is golden and much of the fat has rendered, about 5 minutes. Pour off all but 3 tablespoons of the fat. Add the chili flakes and cook over medium heat for 30 seconds. Add 2 tablespoons water to the pan. Remove from the heat.

CONTINUED

In a large pot of well-salted boiling water, cook the pasta according to the package instructions until 2 minutes shy of al dente; drain.

Toss the mezze maniche into the skillet with the guanciale, butter, and 1 tablespoon of the Pecorino Romano. Cook, stirring occasionally, for 30 seconds. Add the ricotta and cook until the pasta is al dente and a loose, creamy sauce has formed, 1 to 2 minutes. Add more water if necessary.

Divide the pasta among four individual serving plates or bowls and finish each with 1 teaspoon or more of Pecorino and a drizzle of olive oil.

Spaghetti with White Puttanesca

This dish was a happy accident. Andrew was testing a standard—i.e., tomato-based—puttanesca recipe for this book in which he added all the other elements (save the parsley) before the tomato. It looked and smelled gorgeous in the pan, so we tasted it and found it to be fantastic on its own, without the tomatoes.

To bring out the most flavor from these few ingredients, make sure to get your pan extremely hot before attempting to fry the capers and anchovies until they are brown and sizzling. Once the anchovies have dissolved and the capers are nicely crisp, add the garlic and chili flakes, letting them toast and the flavors develop. Really good olives add both some funkiness and some fruitiness, and parsley lends a nice herbal quality to the heady aromas. | **SERVES 4**

½ cup extra-virgin olive oil, plus more for drizzling
8 anchovy fillets
¼ cup salt-packed capers, soaked, drained, and rinsed (see Note, page 43)
1 cup pitted and sliced Nocellara or Cerignola olives

8 fat garlic cloves, smashed and peeled
½ teaspoon chili flakes
1 pound spaghetti
¾ cup chopped flat-leaf parsley
Kosher salt

In a very large skillet (or a Dutch oven; see page 37 for tips), warm ¼ cup of the olive oil over medium-high heat until very hot. Add the anchovies and capers and cook, stirring occasionally, until nicely browned, about 3 minutes. Add the remaining ¼ cup olive oil, the

olives, garlic, and chili flakes and cook until the garlic is golden, about 3 minutes. Add 2 tablespoons water to the pan. Remove from the heat.

In a large pot of well-salted boiling water, cook the pasta according to the package instructions until 2 minutes shy of al dente; drain.

Toss the spaghetti into the skillet with the caper-anchovy mixture. Cook over medium heat until the pasta is al dente, 1 to 2 minutes, adding more water if the sauce seems dry. Toss in the parsley and season with salt to taste.

Divide the pasta among four individual serving plates or bowls and finish each with a drizzle of olive oil.

Note: While we say that good-quality ingredients are important all the time, in this recipe, they are critical. Mushy, bland supermarket Kalamata olives will just not cut it, and this is certainly a dish calling for top-shelf anchovies, and salt-packed capers. If you pull out all the stops, this simple pasta will surprise you.

Rigatoni with Spicy Salami and Tomato

An alternative to a traditional pasta amatriciana (spicy tomato sauce made with cured pork guanciale), this soul-satisfying dish was born thanks to a test batch of salami that we made for our provisions shop, Bklyn Larder. Somehow we'd gotten the chili proportions off and while it wasn't spicy enough to sell as sopressata, it was too spicy to sell as regular salami. So Andrew sliced the salami up, crisped it in a pan, and added our house tomato sauce and plenty of olive oil and cheese. It's a simple dish with lusty, soul-satisfying flavors, bolstered with lots of chili. | **SERVES 4**

8 ounces spicy sopressata, casings removed

2 tablespoons extra-virgin olive oil, plus more for drizzling

½ teaspoon chili flakes

2 cups Basic Tomato Sauce (recipe follows)

1 pound rigatoni

¼ cup finely grated Pecorino Romano, plus more for serving

Cut the sopressata into batons about 2 inches long and ¼ inch thick.

In a very large skillet (or a Dutch oven; see page 37 for tips), warm the olive oil over medium-high heat. Add the sopressata and cook, stirring occasionally, until it has crisped and rendered some of its fat. Add the chili flakes and cook for 30 seconds, then add the tomato sauce and cook over high heat until most of the liquid has evaporated, about 8 minutes. Remove from the heat.

CONTINUED

In a large pot of well-salted boiling water, cook the pasta according to the package instructions until 2 minutes shy of al dente; drain.

Toss the rigatoni into the skillet with the sopressata and tomato mixture and cook over medium heat, stirring occasionally, until the pasta is al dente and the sauce has reduced and clings to the pasta, 2 to 3 minutes. Add the Pecorino Romano, then add a few tablespoons of water if the sauce seems dry.

Divide the pasta among four individual serving plates or bowls and finish each with a sprinkling of Pecorino and a drizzle of olive oil.

Basic Tomato Sauce

MAKES 2 CUPS

¼ cup extra-virgin olive oil
½ yellow onion, chopped
1 garlic clove, thinly sliced
½ teaspoon kosher salt, plus
more to taste

Freshly cracked black pepper
One 28-ounce can San Marzano
or other good-quality plum
tomatoes

In a medium saucepan, heat the olive oil over medium-low heat. Add the onion, garlic, salt, and a few grinds of pepper and cook, covered, until the vegetables are very soft, 5 to 7 minutes.

Pour in the tomatoes and their liquid, bring to a simmer, and simmer until the sauce thickens and the oil separates and rises to the surface, about 25 minutes.

Run the sauce through a food mill fitted with the large disk (or puree in a food processor). Season with additional salt and pepper as needed. The sauce will keep, in an airtight container, in the refrigerator for 1 week or in the freezer for 3 months.

Fusilli with Pork Sausage Ragu

This is one of the most popular dishes at Franny's. Instead of taking big cuts of meat and braising them until they fall apart, we grind the meat and aggressively season it, thereby making a kind of ad hoc sausage meat. The flavor notes here are very much those of Southern Italy, with a touch of rich tomato paste and a dash of chili. Pancetta, with its porky richness, adds another dimension. Fusilli, offering up all those nooks and crannies in which the sausage can hide, makes the perfect companion to this ragu. | **SERVES 4 TO 6**

2 tablespoons unsalted butter

2 tablespoons extra-virgin olive oil

2½ pounds coarsely ground pork

⅔ cup ¼-inch-diced pancetta (3½ ounces)

½ teaspoon chili flakes

3 large garlic cloves, minced

1 medium onion, minced

⅔ cup finely diced carrots

⅔ cup finely diced celery

2⅔ cup chopped flat-leaf parsley

3½ tablespoons tomato paste

⅔ cup dry red wine

One 14-ounce can Italian cherry tomatoes, drained and smashed, or canned diced tomatoes

2 cups water

2 teaspoons kosher salt, plus more to taste

Freshly cracked black pepper

1 pound fusilli

Finely grated Parmigiano-Reggiano and fresh ricotta for finishing

In a heavy stockpot or a Dutch oven, melt the butter with the olive oil over medium-high heat. Add the ground pork (cook in batches if necessary) and cook just until golden; be careful not to overbrown. Using a slotted spoon, remove the meat from the pot and set aside.

CONTINUED

Add the pancetta to the pot and cook gently over medium heat until the fat is rendered and the meat begins to crisp. Stir in the chili flakes and garlic and cook until fragrant, about 1 minute. Add the onion, carrots, celery, and parsley and cook until the onion is translucent, 10 to 15 minutes. Stir in the tomato paste and cook for 2 minutes, then add the red wine and bring to a simmer.

Add the pork to the pot, along with the tomatoes, water, and salt. Bring the mixture to a simmer, cover the pot with a tight-fitting lid, and simmer for 40 minutes.

Remove the lid and continue to simmer until the ragu has thickened nicely, 15 to 20 minutes longer. Season to taste with salt and pepper. Let the ragu cool to room temperature, then refrigerate until thoroughly chilled.

Remove and discard about two-thirds of the fat that has settled on the surface of the ragu, leaving the remaining third to be incorporated back into the sauce.

In a large pot of well-salted boiling water, cook the pasta according to the package instructions until 2 minutes shy of al dente; drain.

While the pasta is cooking, in a very large skillet (or a Dutch oven; see page 37 for tips), warm the ragu over medium heat.

Toss the fusilli into the skillet with the ragu and cook until al dente, 1 to 2 minutes. If the sauce seems dry, add a few tablespoons of water.

Divide the pasta among four individual serving plates or bowls. Finish each with a sprinkle of Parmigiano-Reggiano and a dollop of ricotta.

Linguine with Bottarga di Muggine

Bottarga, the pressed dried roe of certain fish, is a fabulous Italian pantry item that is underappreciated in the United States. It keeps forever and adds a unique richness and brininess to whatever you use it with. We like to use mullet bottarga, as it's milder and more delicate than tuna bottarga. The mullet roe has a delicate salinity, a hint of bitterness, and a touch of sweetness that pairs really well with buttery noodles.

Bottarga is easy to use; just shave some on the top of your pasta, and it will meld into the sauce, imparting a sea-salty taste. The heat and steam of the noodles blooms the flavors of bottarga. Use a fine Microplane zester, which will get the bottarga almost powdery: the more surface area you expose, the more aromatics you'll gain. | **SERVES 4**

1 pound linguine

2 tablespoons unsalted butter

½ teaspoon freshly cracked
   black pepper

Juice of 1½ lemons, or
   more to taste

⅔ cup finely grated
   bottarga di muggine
   (see Resources, page 89)

About 4 teaspoons extra-virgin
   olive oil

In a large pot of well-salted boiling water, cook the pasta according to the package instructions until 2 minutes shy of al dente; drain.

Meanwhile, in a very large skillet (or a Dutch oven; see page 37 for tips), combine 2 tablespoons water, the butter, and the pepper and stir over medium-high heat until the butter has melted. Add the pasta, toss to coat, and cook until the pasta is al dente, 1 to

2 minutes, adding more water if the pasta seems dry. Stir in the lemon juice.

Divide the pasta among four individual serving plates or bowls and finish each with about 2½ tablespoons of the grated bottarga and about 1 teaspoon olive oil; sprinkle on more lemon juice if needed.

Linguine with Meyer Lemon

Pairing lemon with pasta is just brilliant, as it lightens up what could be a very heavy dish. While the Northern Italian rendition uses a mix of cream and lemon juice, this has a silky butter sauce made with lemon zest as well as juice—it's a bright, clean-flavored, lemony pasta. Serve this in winter, when sweet, thin-skinned Meyer lemons are available and you start craving a comforting yet sunny-tasting dish like this. But don't sweat it if you don't have Meyer lemons; regular lemon sweetened with a squeeze of tangerine works beautifully in their place (see the variation).

We add a drizzle of olive oil—ideally a light, aromatic Ligurian oil—just before serving so that the fragrance of the warmed oil melds with the sauce. Our kids beg for this: when she was only two years old, our daughter, Prue, used to shout, "More lemon!" | **SERVES 4**

1 pound linguine
6 tablespoons unsalted butter
½ teaspoon freshly cracked black pepper
Finely grated zest of 2 Meyer lemons
¼ cup finely grated Parmigiano-Reggiano, plus more if desired
Juice of 1 Meyer lemon
½ teaspoon kosher salt, or more to taste
Extra-virgin olive oil

In a large pot of well-salted boiling water, cook the pasta according to the package instructions until 2 minutes shy of al dente; drain.

In a very large skillet (or a Dutch oven; see page 37 for tips) set over medium-low heat, combine the linguine and ¼ cup water. Stir in the butter, pepper, and lemon zest. Increase the heat to medium and use a pair of tongs to toss the pasta. If the pasta seems dry, add a little more water. Stir in the cheese, lemon juice, and salt; toss again and cook until the sauce has thickened slightly and only a little liquid remains in the pan and the pasta is al dente (increase the heat to high if necessary).

Divide the pasta among four individual serving plates or bowls and finish each with a drizzle of olive oil and more cheese, if desired.

Variation

Linguine with Lemon and Tangerine: Substitute the zest of 1 regular lemon and 1 tangerine for the Meyer lemon zest and the juice of ½ lemon and ½ tangerine for the Meyer lemon juice.

Farro Spaghetti with Anchovies, Chilies, and Garlic

Pasta made from whole-grain farro (an heirloom grain that is a close cousin to wheat) is richer, nuttier, and earthier than that made from regular wheat flour. This is a perfect winter dish; farro's heft and body will feel comforting and fortifying. Originally we based this dish on a pasta with anchovies and walnuts we'd eaten in Naples. But because the farro itself was nutty, we ended up nixing the walnuts, though we kept the anchovies and brightened everything with a squeeze of lemon and some spicy chili. If you can't find farro pasta, you can use whole wheat pasta in its place. | **SERVES 4**

½ cup extra-virgin olive oil, plus
   more for drizzling
8 garlic cloves, smashed and
   peeled
10 anchovy fillets
½ teaspoon chili flakes
1 pound farro spaghetti (or use
   whole wheat)

⅓ cup chopped flat-leaf parsley
¼ teaspoon freshly cracked
   black pepper
Juice of ½ lemon
2 to 3 tablespoons finely grated
   Pecorino Romano

In a very large skillet (or a Dutch oven; see page 37 for tips), heat the olive oil over medium-high heat. Stir in the garlic and anchovies and cook until the anchovies are dissolved and the garlic is beginning to color, 2 to 3 minutes. Add the chili flakes and cook for about 30 seconds. Add 2 tablespoons water to the pan. Remove from the heat.

CONTINUED

In a large pot of well-salted boiling water, cook the pasta according to the package instructions until 2 minutes shy of al dente; drain.

Toss the spaghetti into the skillet with the garlic-anchovy mixture, parsley, and pepper. Cook over medium heat until the pasta is al dente, 1 to 2 minutes. Stir in the lemon juice and a little more water if the pasta seems dry.

Divide the pasta among four individual serving plates or bowls and finish each with a sprinkle of Pecorino Romano and a drizzle of olive oil.

Resources

Italian Pantry Items

Salt-packed capers from Pantelleria, pasta, high-quality anchovies, bottarga, excellent olive oils, San Marzano tomatoes

bklynlarder.com
buonitalia.com
gustiamo.com

Dried Herbs and Spices

Fennel seeds, bay leaves, and more

bklynlarder.com
kalustyans.com
madecasse.com
manicaretti.com
thespicehouse.com

Heritage Meats

heritagefoodsusa.com
nimanranch.com

Flours

Premium flours, including durum, "00" pasta flour, and all-purpose

kingarthurflour.com

Index

Conversion Charts

Here are rounded-off equivalents between the metric system and the traditional systems that are used in the United States to measure weight and volume.

FRACTIONS — DECIMALS

FRACTIONS	DECIMALS
⅛	.125
¼	.25
⅓	.33
⅜	.375
½	.5
⅝	.625
⅔	.67
¾	.75
⅞	.875

WEIGHTS

US/UK	METRIC
¼ oz	7 g
½ oz	15 g
1 oz	30 g
2 oz	55 g
3 oz	85 g
4 oz	110 g
5 oz	140 g
6 oz	170 g
7 oz	200 g
8 oz (½ lb)	225 g
9 oz	250 g
10 oz	280 g
11 oz	310 g
12 oz	340 g
13 oz	370 g
14 oz	400 g
15 oz	425 g
16 oz (1 lb)	455 g

VOLUME

AMERICAN	IMPERIAL	METRIC
¼ tsp		1.25 ml
½ tsp		2.5 ml
1 tsp		5 ml
½ Tbsp (1½ tsp)		7.5 ml
1 Tbsp (3 tsp)		15 ml
¼ cup (4 Tbsp)	2 fl oz	60 ml
⅓ cup (5 Tbsp)	2½ fl oz	75 ml
½ cup (8 Tbsp)	4 fl oz	125 ml
⅔ cup (10 Tbsp)	5 fl oz	150 ml
¾ cup (12 Tbsp)	6 fl oz	175 ml
1 cup (16 Tbsp)	8 fl oz	250 ml
1¼ cups	10 fl oz	300 ml
1½ cups	12 fl oz	350 ml
2 cups (1 pint)	16 fl oz	500 ml
2½ cups	20 fl oz (1 pint)	625 ml
5 cups	40 fl oz (1 qt)	1.25 l

OVEN TEMPERATURES

	°F	°C	GAS MARK
very cool	250–275	130–140	½–1
cool	300	148	2
warm	325	163	3
moderate	350	177	4
moderately hot	375–400	190–204	5–6
hot	425	218	7
very hot	450–475	232–245	8–9

°C/F TO °F/C CONVERSION CHART

°C/F	°C	°F	°C/F	°C	°F	°C/F	°C	°F	°C/F	°C	°F
90	32	194	220	104	428	350	177	662	480	249	896
100	38	212	230	110	446	360	182	680	490	254	914
110	43	230	240	116	464	370	188	698	500	260	932
120	49	248	250	121	482	380	193	716	510	266	950
130	54	266	260	127	500	390	199	734	520	271	968
140	60	284	270	132	518	400	204	752	530	277	986
150	66	302	280	138	536	410	210	770	540	282	1,004
160	71	320	290	143	554	420	216	788	550	288	1,022
170	77	338	300	149	572	430	221	806			
180	82	356	310	154	590	440	227	824			
190	88	374	320	160	608	450	232	842			
200	93	392	330	166	626	460	238	860			
210	99	410	340	171	644	470	243	878			

Example: If your temperature is 90°F, your conversion is 32°C; if your temperature is 90°C, your conversion is 194°F.

Library of Congress Cataloging-in-Publication Data

Names: Feinberg, Andrew, 1974– author. | Stephens, Francine, author. | Clark, Melissa, author.
Title: The artisanal kitchen : perfect pasta / Andrew Feinberg, Francine Stephens, Melissa Clark.
Description: New York, NY : Artisan, a division of Workman Publishing Company, Inc. [2017]
Identifiers: LCCN 2016032081 | ISBN 9781579657628 (hardback, paper over board)
Subjects: LCSH: Cooking (Pasta)–Italy. | Seasonal cooking–Italy. | Cooking, Italian. | LCGFT: Cookbooks.
Classification: LCC TX809.M17 F45 2017 | DDC 641.82/20945–dc23
LC record available at https://lccn.loc.gov/2016032081

Artisan books are available at special discounts when purchased in bulk for premiums and sales promotions as well as for fund-raising or educational use. Special editions or book excerpts also can be created to specification. For details, contact the Special Sales Director at the address below, or send an e-mail to specialmarkets@workman.com.

Published by Artisan
A division of Workman Publishing Co., Inc.
225 Varick Street
New York, NY 10014-4381
artisanbooks.com

Artisan is a registered trademark of Workman Publishing Co., Inc.

Portions of this book have been adapted from material that appears in *Franny's: Simple Seasonal Italian* (Artisan, 2013).

Published simultaneously in Canada by Thomas Allen & Son, Limited

Printed in China
First printing, May 2017

10 9 8 7 6 5 4 3 2 1